# Backbiting and Its Harmful Effects on Muslims

## Husayn al-Awayishah

# Table of Contents

**Introduction**

# Introduction

Praise be to Allaah; we praise Him and seek His help and forgiveness. We seek refuge in Him from the evil of our own souls and actions. Whomever Allaah guides, none can lead astray, and whomever Allaah leaves astray, none can guide. I bear witness that there is no god but Allaah Alone, who has no partner, and I bear witness that Muhammad is His slave and Messenger.

"O you who believe! Fear Allaah as He should be feared, and die only in a state of Islam."

(Al 'Imran 3: 102)

"O mankind! Reverence your Guardian-Lord, Who created you from a single person, created, of the same nature, his spouse, and from them two spread (as seeds) innumerable men and women; - fear Allaah, through whom you claim your mutual (rights) and (reverence) the womb (that bore you): for Allaah is always watching over you."

[al-Nisa' 4: 1]

"O you who believe! Fear Allaah, and say (always) a word directed to the Right: that He may make your conduct whole and sound and forgive you your sins: he who obeys Allaah and His Apostle has already attained the highest achievement."

[al-Ahzab 33:70-71)

The most truthful speech is the Book of Allaah and the best guidance is the guidance of Muhammad (peace and blessings of Allaah be upon him). The worst affairs are the ones that are made up. Everything that is fabricated is an innovation (*Bid'ah*); every innovation is a going-astray, and every going-astray leads to the fire of hell.

When I thought of people's tongues, it was like they were burning flames or poisonous snakes! How much grief, sorrow and evil they cause!

So I decided to write a book on this matter, seeking to serve the pleasure of Allaah (THE MOST HIGH) and to protect and help the Muslims - first by explaining the dangers and evils of the tongue, and the sorrow, grief and regret that it can cause in this world and the next; and then by showing how these problems can be avoided, *in sha' Allaah.*

I wrote many chapters. Indeed, years passed and I still hadn't finished the project. I was burdened with other work obligations until Allaah (THE MOST HIGH) made it easier for me to complete the research. I wrote about all the evil results that can come from people's tongues under the title Hasa'id al -Alsun (Harvest of Tongues). However, I felt that it would be more useful to deal with the subject of *al-Gheebah* (gossip, backbiting) by focusing on it and writing a book solely on this subject, which is what I have done - wa ma Tawfiqi illa Billah (and in Allaah Alone is my success).

I would like to express my deepest gratitude to everyone who helped in the production of this book, above all to my Shaykh Muhammad Nasir al-Din al-Albani (May Allaah preserve him), who let me use everything I needed on this subject from his valuable *MS Sahih al-Targhib wa'l-Tarhib* and various other books and studies. May Allaah (THE MOST HIGH) reward him with good on my behalf and on behalf of all the Muslims.

I ask Allaah (THE MOST HIGH) to benefit me from this work and that it may be a witness for me and not against me (on the Day of Judgment). Indeed, He is able to do everything.

# Texts stating the prohibition of Gheebah

"... Nor speak evil of one another behind their backs. Would any of you like to eat the flesh of his dead brother? Nay, you would abhor it... But fear Allaah: for Allaah Oft-Returning, Most Merciful."

[al -Hujurat 49:12]

On the authority of al-Muttalib ibn 'Abdullah, who said: The Messenger of Allaah (peace and blessings of Allaah be upon him) said: "Gheebah (gossip, backbiting) means that a man mentions about a person something that is true behind his back."

From Abu Hurayrah (Allaah be pleased with him): The Messenger of Allaah (peace and blessings of Allaah be upon him) said: "Do you know what Gheebah is?" They said: "Allaah and His Messenger know best." He said: "(It is that) you mention something about your brother that he does not like."

From Abu Barzah al-Aslami and al-Bara' ibn 'Azib who said: The Messenger of Allaah (peace and blessings of Allaah be upon him) said:

"O people who pay lip-service to the Faith when it has not entered your hearts! Do not gossip about the Muslims and do not expose their faults. Whoever reveals the fault of his Muslim brother, Allaah will reveal his fault, and if Allaah reveals his fault, it will be open for all to see, even if he hid in the innermost part of his house."

## What is al-Gheebah?

It is clear from the above that Gheebah means to say something about a person which is true but which he does not like, behind his back.

# Consensus among the scholars on the prohibition of Gheebah and on the fact that it is a major sin

Ibn Katheer, Allaah have mercy on him, said in his Tafseer of Surah al-Hujurat: "Gheebah is forbidden by consensus (Ijma'), and in general there is no exception to it, except in circumstances where it is necessary to speak about people, such as al-Jarh wa'l- Ta'dil (establishing the status and authenticity of Hadeeth narrators) and al-Naseehah (giving advice)."

Al-Qurtubi said: "The scholars agree that it is a major sin and that committing this sin necessitates repentance (Tawbah) to Allaah (THE MOST HIGH)."

This is evident from the words of Allaah (THE MOST HIGH):

"... Would any of you like to eat the flesh of his dead brother? No, you would abhor it..."

[al-Hujurat 49:12]

Indications that Gheebah is a major sin are also found in the following Ahadith:

"What is worse than usury (*Riba*) is that a man insults his brother's honor."

And the words of the Prophet (peace and blessings of Allaah be upon him) to 'A'ishah (Allaah be pleased with her):

"You have spoken a word which, if it could be mixed with the waters of the sea, it would have been." [that is, the extent of it is such that even if it were mixed with the great waters of the sea, it would not be hidden at all]

# Common but invalid excuses for Gheebah

Shaytan comes to people in many ways to tempt them to backbite or gossip:

(A) He says to some of them: What you say behind the person's back is true, so there is nothing wrong with it.

But this is forbidden by the sayings of the Prophet (peace and blessings of Allaah be upon him), such as the following:

(1) The two Ahadeeth mentioned above (in the previous chapter):

(a) "Gheebah means that a man mentions something about a person which is true behind his back."

(b) Hadeeth from Abu Hurayrah (Allaah be pleased with him): The Messenger of Allaah (peace and blessings of Allaah be upon him) said: "Do you know what Gheebah is?" They said: "Allaah and His Messenger know best."

He said: "(It is that) you mention something about your brother that he does not like."

Someone asked: "What if what I say about my brother is true?"

He said: "If what you say is true, then this is gossip (Gheebah); and if it is not true, then it is slander."

(2) Ahadith quoted in al-Ahadith al- Mukhtarah , from the report of al-Diya' al-Maqdisi, from Anas ibn Malik, who said: The Arabs used to serve each other on their journeys. Abu Bakr and 'Umar had with them a man who used to serve them. (One day) they woke up and (found that) he had not prepared any food for them. One said to the other: "This one sleeps as if he were at home!" [i.e., criticizing him for sleeping too long]. So they woke him up and said to him: "Go to the Messenger of Allaah (peace and blessings of Allaah be upon him) and say to him: 'Abu Bakr and 'Umar send you salaams and wish to ask you for some food."

He (peace and blessings of Allaah be upon him) said, "They have eaten." They were astonished to hear this, so they came to the Prophet (peace and blessings of Allaah be upon him) and said, "O Messenger of Allaah! We sent to you to request for food, and you said we had eaten. What have we eaten?" He said, "Your brother's flesh. By him in whose hand my soul is, I can see his flesh between your teeth." They said: "Ask forgiveness for us." He said, "Let him ask forgiveness for you!"

When they said "This one sleeps as if he were at home!", it was true, but the Prophet (peace and blessings of Allaah be upon him) told them that they had eaten of his flesh.

People must be careful about eating their brother's flesh! - like saying: How often does so-and-so take a bath.' How much he eats.' How evil he is! How much he sleeps!

(B) Some people will say: We are saying this behind his back for his own benefit, although he does not know what is good for him! They might even say: We are doing this in the interest of society as a whole.

These claims can be rejected on several counts:

(1) Any action that is performed must be performed in accordance with the Shari'ah. Good intentions alone, without regard to anything else, will not be sufficient to save a person from the wrath of Allaah. In fact, the Mushrikun (pagans) claimed to have the best of intentions, but Allaah (THE MOST HIGH) made their status very clear in the Qur'an when He said:

> But those who take protectors other than Allaah
> (say): 'We serve them only that they may bring us
> nearer to Allaah'
>
> [al-Zumar 39:3]

They may have had this lofty intention – to be brought closer to Allaah (THE MOST HIGH) – but that did not stop the Prophet (peace and blessings of Allaah be upon him) and his noble companions (Allaah be pleased with them) from fighting them.

Doing good deeds in the interest of an individual or society cannot be achieved by backbiting people or spreading gossip about their private affairs!

(2) If the claims are true and said with the right intention, then the method of acting upon those intentions must also be sound.

This is best achieved by speaking directly to the person and encouraging him, with gentle wisdom, to adhere to the teachings of Islam and avoid following his own whims. This advice and encouragement may need to be repeated, but if this does not produce any results, look for someone else to give this advice because your approach may not have worked. Ask the person you are approaching to keep secret whatever you tell him about that person. He should choose the most appropriate way to address the person, directly or indirectly. If you find that the person will not give up his shameful deed or sin, even after repeatedly counseling him, then all you can do is to leave him alone who commits his sin in secret, and do not disclose it to anyone. If you reveal it, you will have caused many problems in the Muslim community, including the following:

(a) you will have transgressed the texts which command us to cover the faults of a fellow Muslim.

(b) you will have spread doubt, thereby making Muslims suspicious of even the best among them, and making it harder for them to trust each other.

(c) you will have caused the Muslims to start gossiping about each other and spreading hatred among them, thereby distracting them from the pressing matters before them and the community and the Ummah as a whole.

(d) you will have pushed him who had committed his sin in secret to openly commit his sin.

3 - Any intelligent person will accept that there can be no benefit to the Muslim community in backbiting a person who tries to hide his faults and sins. What possible benefit can there be in such talk?! What good can this do the Muslim Ummah - liberate Jerusalem?! Or destroy Shirk and Mushrikin?!

4 - Not only can the backbiting fail to achieve the purported purposes - whether at the individual or community level - but the victim can begin to hate those who spoke about him in his absence, until the situation worsens, as the poet described:

"There is no bond of blood or friendship (between us): the gulf is too wide to be bridged."

# Some of the motives for Gheebah and the Islamic response to them

1- Getting things off the chest [especially in the case of hate]:

A person may do something to upset another, and whenever the aggrieved person feels angry about it, he will get it off his chest by telling his friend about it. To avoid doing this, we should remember the words of Allaah (THE MOST HIGH):

"Be swift in the race for forgiveness from your Lord and for a garden the width of which is (whole) of the heavens and the earth, prepared for the righteous, - those who spend (freely), whether they are in prosperity or in adversity; who restrains anger and forgives (all) men; - For Allaah loves those who do good."

[Al 'Imran 3: 133-134]

And the Hadeeth of the Messenger of Allaah (peace and blessings of Allaah be upon him): "Whoever controls his anger, even if he is able to act on it, Allaah will call him before all people on the Day of Judgment and invite him to choose whom he wishes of al-Hur al -'Ayn."

He who gossips to "get something off his chest" is not considered to be one who has controlled his anger.

2 - Being in with a group of friends.

When a group engages in the discussion of people's honor, a person may think that if he speaks out and tries to stop them, they will dislike him and exclude him. So he joins them, believing that this is what good company is like.

But we should remember the words of the Messenger of Allaah (peace and blessings of Allaah be upon him): "Whoever seeks the approval of the people by angering Allaah, Allaah will leave him to the people."

3 - Seeking to raise one's own status by putting others down.

In this case, a person may say, "So-and-so is ignorant, he is not wise..." etc. By doing this, he seeks to prove that he is better and that he knows better.

We should remind ourselves that what is with Allaah (THE MOST HIGH) is better and is eternal and that this world is not worth even a gnat's wing in the sight of Allaah. This person may be better than you in the sight of Allaah (THE MOST HIGH), as in the Hadeeth: "Perhaps this scruffy man, who has closed doors in his face, if he swore an oath to Allaah and asked him for something, Allaah would do it for him!" [Muslim, Ahmad].

4- Fooling around and joking.

One person can mention another in such a way that this makes people laugh - some people even make their living this way.

But we have to remember the words of the Prophet (peace and blessings of Allaah be upon him): "Woe to him who lies to make the people laugh - woe to him, woe to him!"

5 - Jealousy.

It may be the case that a person may be praised in an assembly where he is well-liked by the people, and a jealous person may hear this. The jealous one then insults the other so that the latter may lose the status he previously enjoyed.

I have discussed the answer to this problem in Amrad yu'ani minha al-Hasidun bi-Alsunatihim (The diseases suffered by those who reap the harvest of their tongue).

The jealous person should remember that because of his jealousy and insults, the person who is the object of his envy will be above, not only in this world, but on the Day of Resurrection.

6 - If a person has been accused of doing something, he will mention the name of the one who actually did it in order to clear his own name, thinking that this is the best way; or else he will mention someone else who

participated in the deed, hoping thus to excuse himself by saying "so-and-so did it, and so-and-so did it too."

The person has the right to protest his innocence, but he does not have the right to name the person who did the deed or others who participated in it.

7 - Anger for the sake of Allaah (THE MOST HIGH).

A person may become angry because of a sin committed by another person, so he talks about it, demonstrates his anger and mentions that person's name when he should have hidden that person's name and not mentioned him in this way.

8 - A man may feel sorry for his brother because he is going through some difficulties, so he mentions him by name and says, "Poor so-and-so, he is really going through a bad time!" He may be sincere in that which he says, but it is wrong of him to mention the name of the person he is talking about.

In this case, we should remember the words of Allaah (THE MOST HIGH):

"Then whoever has done an atom's weight of good shall see it! And whoever has done an atom's weight of evil shall see it."

[al- Zalzalah 99:7-8]

How much evil is due to the gossip of the Muslims! A good intention does not justify an evil deed, as we have explained above. A person will be rewarded for his intention, but he is considered a sinner because of his deed.

A person who has too much free time and is bored may find nothing better to spend his time than talking about people and their faults and mentioning things they don't like.

To combat this, we should fill our leisure time with worthwhile activities and worship and the pursuit of knowledge; we should remind ourselves of the words of the Prophet (peace and blessings of Allaah be upon him):

"The son of Adam will not be dismissed by his Lord on the Day of Resurrection until he has been asked about five things: his life and how he spent it; his youth and how he spent it; his wealth and how he earned it, and what he used it for and what he did with the knowledge he got."

10 - A man may seek to get closer to his superiors by criticizing his colleagues in order to gain promotion or make them think well of him.

The Muslim should remember the Ayat and Ahadith which speak of Rizq (sustenance) and that no harm or benefit can befall him except by the permission of Allaah (THE MOST HIGH). Belief in al-Qadr (predestination) is the basis for combating this problem.

Therefore , I will remind such people of the Hadeeth of the Messenger of Allaah (peace and blessings of Allaah be upon him): "Whoever seeks to gain the approval of the people by angering Allaah, Allaah will leave him to the people."

11 - Conceit and lack of awareness of one's faults.

The answer to this is the opposite: a person should think about his mistakes, try to correct them and be ashamed to criticize someone else when he himself has mistakes.

The Messenger of Allaah (peace and blessings of Allaah be upon him) condemned conceit and said: "If you were not to sin, I would fear something even worse for you: conceit, conceit!"

# Ahadeeth aimed to deter people from Gossip

From Abi Bakrah (Allaah be pleased with him): The Messenger of Allaah (peace and blessings of Allaah be upon him) said in his sermon during the Farewell Pilgrimage: "Your blood, your wealth and your honor are sacred, as this day of yours, in this month of yours, in this land of yours are sacred. Have I not told you?"

Let us think deeply about this and regard the orders of Allaah (THE MOST HIGH) and His Prophet (peace and blessings of Allaah be upon him) with the reverence they deserve.

In the eyes of Allaah, violating your brother's rights by gossiping is tantamount to violating the sanctity of Yawm al -Nahr (the Day of Sacrifice), in the month of Dhu'l -Hijjah in Mina. Are you not aware of the extent of this violation of a Muslim's honor, you who slander and gossip and eat the flesh of Muslims?!

On the authority of al-Bara' ibn 'Azib (Allaah be pleased with him), who said: The Messenger of Allaah (peace and blessings of Allaah be upon him) said: "There are seventy-two degrees of Riba (usury), the least of which is equivalent to committing adultery with one's own mother. The worst of them is that a man insults his brother's honor."

Allaah is great (Allaahu akbar)! Where is our reason? Allaah is great! Where is the faith that should fill our hearts? Where is the faith that should control the whims and desires of the self? Where is the faith that will prevent us from insulting the honor of our fellow Muslims?

Riba is a serious sin! The matter is considered to be of such enormous magnitude that Allaah (THE MOST HIGH) declared war on whoever engages in it. The lowest degree of Riba corresponds to a man committing adultery with his own mother, but the worst type of Riba is a man insulting his brother's honor.

Do not you understand?!

So - go ahead and insult your brother's honor to your heart's content; backbite, spread rumors, insult and criticize... but where will you run on the Day of Resurrection?!

On the authority of 'A'ishah (Allaah be pleased with her), who said: I said to the Prophet (peace and blessings of Allaah be upon him): "It is bad enough that Safiyyah is..." (Some of the narrators said: she meant that she was short). He said, "You have spoken a word which, if it could be mixed with the waters of the sea, it would have been. [i.e., the extent of it is such that even if it were mixed with the great waters of the sea, it would not be hidden at all]

A word which, if it could be mixed with the water of the sea, it would have been!! One word alone could do this, and have such a far-reaching effect! So what do you think of today's gossip whose tongues never stop wagging? What great oceans could be stained and corrupted by their words! How many quiet lives are disturbed by them!

From 'Amr ibn Shu'ayb from his father from his grandfather: (the people) mentioned a man to the Messenger of Allaah (peace and blessings of Allaah be upon him) who said: "He does not eat until he is full, and he does not visit anyone until they have visited him first." The Prophet (peace and blessings of Allaah be upon him) said: "You have gossiped about him." They said: "O Messenger of Allaah! We have mentioned something about him which is true."

He said:

"It's bad enough that you mentioned something about your brother that is true."

We should all ask ourselves: who among us is infallible? Who has made his Qarin submit in Islam? Who among us is free from mistakes, errors and sins? Who among us would be content to have everything about him, good and bad, talked about by others?

Any one of us becomes enraged if he hears any insinuation of him; so what would you do if it was said clearly and in detail, let alone behind your back?

From Anas (Allaah be pleased with him), who said: The Messenger of Allaah (peace and blessings of Allaah be upon him) said: "When I was taken up to heaven, I passed by people who had copper claws tearing into their faces and breasts. I asked: 'Who are these, O Jibril?' He said: They are the ones who ate the flesh of the people and insulted their honor.

Have these gossips lost their minds? How can they continue to insult the honor of Muslims and eat their flesh after hearing this hadith? Let them have the glad tidings of copper claws tearing at their faces and breasts! These claws are far worse than the claws of the wild beasts, to sharpen the punishment for their evil deeds. So it's up to you to decide how much you want to indulge in gossip after reading this!

On the authority of 'Abdullah ibn Mas'ud (Allaah be pleased with him), who said: We were with the Prophet (peace and blessings of Allaah be upon him) when a man got up and left, whereupon another man immediately began to backbite him. The Prophet (peace and blessings of Allaah be upon him) said: "Clean the pieces of meat between your teeth!" He said: "What shall I clean between my teeth? I have not eaten any meat!" He said: "You have eaten your brother's flesh!"

Such is the state of our society today: any one of us can commit the sin of gossip or backbiting, but will then say: I did not gossip, I did not eat meat, I did nothing!

Why?!

Because we have allowed our tongues to get used to speaking in this way, without knowing what Gheebah is.

Let's learn about our religion. Let's learn about Halaal and Haraam - as much as we can - and distinguish between the speech that is Halaal and the speech that is Haraam.

# The prohibition on listening to gossip

Allaah (THE MOST HIGH) said:

"... Every act of hearing, or seeing, or (feeling in) the heart will be enquired into (on the Day of Reckoning)."

[al- lsraa' 17 :36 ]

If Satan ever makes you forget, then after recollection do not sit with those who do wrong."

[al-An'am 6:68)

"And when they hear vain talk, they turn away from therefrom..."

[al-Qasas 28:55]

From Ka'b ibn Malik, in the long Hadeeth concerning his repentance; he said: The Prophet (peace and blessings of Allaah be upon him) said when he was sitting among the people of Tabuk: "What happened to Ka'b ibn Malik?" A man from Banu Salamah said: "O Messenger of Allaah, the beauty of his cloak and the appreciation of his sides (have detained him)!" Mu'adh ibn Jabal said: "Woe to what you have said. By Allaah, O Messenger of Allaah, we know nothing but good about him."

The Messenger of Allaah (peace and blessings of Allaah be upon him) remained silent.

What do we learn from these texts?

1 - Listening to and paying attention to gossip is something for which the individual will have to answer to Allaah (THE MOST HIGH).

2 - That it is forbidden to sit with people who are gossiping and backbiting.

3 - Refusing to listen to Gheebah and bad speech is one of the qualities of the believer.

The Hadeeth which narrated the story of Ka'b (Allaah be pleased with him) goes beyond the rejection of Gheebah : The Muslim 's honor should be defended by criticizing what the gossip says and by saying something good about the person which is true. Thus Mu'adh (Allaah be pleased with him) said to the gossip: "Woe to what you have said. By Allaah, O Messenger of Allaah, we know nothing about him but good."

The Prophet (peace and blessings of Allaah be upon him) said: "Whoever defends the honor of his brother, Allaah will protect his face from the Fire on the Day of Resurrection."

The Prophet (peace and blessings of Allaah be upon him) said: "Whoever defends his brother in his absence, Allaah will defend him in this world and the next."

These are matters which are well understood; there is no excuse for any nonsense talk or backbiting.

But anyone who looks at the people today will see them behaving in the opposite way.

You will see them:

1 - To be full of attention of the gossip that criticizes a fellow Muslim;

2 - Listening to it with pleasure, hoping to hear more bad news about the person;

3 - Adding some news or descriptions of their own. To mention something about their brother that he does not like, thus collaborating with Shaytan;

4- Agreeing with the gossip and supporting him in his criticism of the Muslim who is absent.

"Do they not think that they will be called to account?
—on a mighty day, a day when (all) mankind will
stand before the lord of the world?"

[al -Mutaffifin 83:4-6]

The poet described them correctly when he said:

"You would have been heard if you had called people with life in them, but there is no life in those you call.

If you had blown into a fire, it would have flared up, but what you are blowing into is dead ash."

A better description is given in the Qur'an where Allaah (THE MOST HIGH) says:

"The same applies to them, whether you exhort them or whether you exhort them not: they will not believe."

[YaSin 36: 10]

One of the verses of the poem about the prohibition of listening to gossip says:

"Guard your ears from listening to evil speech,
just as you would guard your tongue from speaking it.
For when you listen to evil speech,
You are an accomplice of the one speaking - so beware!"

# The one who listens to Gossip and the gossiper is the same

Remember the Hadeeth of Anas (Allaah be pleased with him) quoted above, in which it was said: "One of them said to his companion: 'This one is sleeping as if he were at home!'

Only one of them said this, but the other listened and agreed with him, so the Prophet (peace and blessings of Allaah be upon him) said to both the speaker and the listener: "You have already eaten!", then he said: "By him in whose hand is my soul, I can see his flesh between your teeth."

# How to stop gossip

If any of us hears gossip about one of our brothers, we are commanded to oppose it and correct the speaker— gently, politely, and with wisdom. This is in accordance with the various ways of changing a bad deed that were described by the Messenger of Allaah (peace and blessings of Allaah be upon him), which we should try to do to the best of our ability. The least of these is to resist the wrong deed in our hearts, which in this case should cause us to leave the assembly where the gossip takes place.

Let us think about the words of Allaah (THE MOST HIGH):

"When you see men engaged in vain talk of Our Signs, turn away from them, unless they turn to some other theme. If Satan ever makes you forget, then after remembrance, do not sit in the company of those who do wrong."

[al-An'am 6:68]

Let those who enjoy gossip beware! The Messenger of Allaah (peace and blessings of Allaah be upon him) ordered those who hear gossip to reject it, but they gladly accept it!

Woe to you! Don't you think about where you will end up? It is as if you think you are only created to fool yourself and commit sins! Tell me for the sake of your Lord: are you Muslims?!

*The hadith reads: "Whoever of you sees an evil deed should change it with his hand [by action], or if he cannot do it, then with his tongue [by speaking out], or if he cannot do it, then with his heart - and that is the weakest of faith." Reported by Muslim (Kitab al-Iman, no. 49).*

# The virtue of speaking up for a Muslim in his absence and opposing Gheebah

Fra Abu'l -Darda' (Allaah be pleased with him):

The Messenger of Allaah (peace and blessings of Allaah be upon him) said: "Whoever defends the honor of his brother, this will be a protection for him from the Fire."

On the authority of Asma' bint Yazid (Allaah be pleased with her), who said: The Prophet (peace and blessings of Allaah be upon him) said: "Whoever defends the honor of his brother in his absence will be entitled to Allaah's protection from the Fire."

The Prophet (peace and blessings of Allaah be upon him) said:

"Whoever defends the honor of his brother, Allaah will protect his face from the Fire of the Day of Resurrection."

From Mu'adh ibn Anas al-Juhani: The Prophet (peace and blessings of Allaah be upon him) said: "Whoever protects a Muslim from a hypocrite, (probably he said:) Allaah will send an angel to protect his flesh from the Fire of Hell; and whoever, who accuses a Muslim of something that seeks to dishonor him,

Allaah will detain him on the bridge of Hell until he
has been fully punished for what he said."

# The stench of those gossiping about the believers

On the authority of Jabir (Allaah be pleased with him), who said: "We were with the Prophet (peace and blessings of Allaah be upon him) when a bad smell came. The Messenger of Allaah (peace and blessings of Allaah be upon him) said: "Do you know what this smell is? This is the stench of those who gossip about the believers."

# The punishment for the gossip in the grave

On the authority of Abu Bakrah (Allaah be pleased with him), who said: While the Prophet (peace and blessings of Allaah be upon him) was walking between me and another man, we came across two graves. He said, "The inhabitants of these graves are being punished, bring me a palm-leaf stalk." Abu Bakrah said: So my companion and I hastened to bring him the palm leaf stalk. He divided it in two and placed one half on each grave, and then said: "May their punishment be mitigated until this dries up, for they are punished for no major sin: they are being punished for gossip and for urinating."

# The person who gossips is a coward with a weak personality

The gossiper is a coward with a weak personality because he cannot confront the person in question. If he was brave, he would tell him to his face and gently point out his mistakes and wrong doings, such as breaking a vow, failing to honor guests properly, or going out with his wife in ways that displease Allaah (THE MOST HIGH).

Why can't we be brave enough to confront a person with his mistakes so that we will earn the reward of enjoining good and forbidding evil and fulfilling the words of Allaah (THE MOST HIGH):

"Who is better in speech than one who calls (men) to Allaah, work righteously and say: 'I am of those who bow in Islam'"

[Fussilat 41:33]

Also, if you confront the person directly, he may become aware of his sins and shortcomings. But if you say the same words behind his back, you yourself will become blameworthy in the eyes of Allaah (THE MOST HIGH) for eating your brother's flesh. If your words get through to the person in question, you don't have a leg to stand on, and you may even resort to lying ("I didn't say that!").

So choose which way you want to go: everyone will go in the direction that will fulfill the purpose for which he was created.

# The gossiper is lacking in Faith

O backbiter, beware! Don't you know you lack faith? Have you not heard the words of the Messenger of Allaah (peace and blessings of Allaah be upon him): "None of you truly believes until he wishes for his brother what he wishes for himself."

Do you really want for your brother what you want for yourself when you gossip about him? Would you like it if someone else said something you don't like behind your back? How can you do something that you would hate to have done to you?

Do you not realize that there is a connection between faith and giving up gossip? Consider the words of the Hadeeth: "None of you truly believes until he wishes for his brother what he wishes for himself." He who wishes for his brother what he wishes for himself has a heart which has been guided; the path of faith has been made easy for him. He who does not do that should think deeply about the Prophet's words: "he does not truly believe."

Think about it: what price do you pay for your enjoyment of gossip?

Faith is the dearest thing a man can possess.

# Gheebah disrupts the commandment of what is good and forbidding what is evil

If we were truly sincere in our Islam and in our deeds, then if we saw someone doing something wrong, we would confront him with his mistake or sin. We would mention it openly and ask him to do right and give up evil.

Whenever (we see someone) doing something wrong and Shaytan comes to tempt us to gossip about it, we should remind ourselves that the deed that he makes so attractive is actually a sin and that the human soul is inclined to do evil deeds that earn the wrath of Allaah (THE MOST HIGH).

One may ask: but what way is there for the heart that is overwhelmed with frustration due to man's constant shortcomings and sins? But we know that the religion of Allaah (Deen) is one of ease and mercy: this frustration can therefore be channeled to make a person better and more obedient to Allaah (THE MOST HIGH).

So go to the one who commits the sin or who has the deficiency and get it all out of your chest - as long as you do this purely for the sake of Allaah (THE MOST

HIGH). Speak softly and wisely, and explain to him that you do this because you want for him what you want for yourself; leave nothing unsaid in your heart.

Go back to Him every time you see the sin or deficiency repeated. Continue enjoining the right and forbidding the evil. By doing this you will be one of the best peoples developed for mankind.

Have you not read the words of Allaah (THE MOST HIGH)?

"You are the best of people, produced (as an example) for mankind. You enjoin what is right, forbid what is wrong, and believe in Allaah..." [Al 'Imran 3: 110]

But we can see that most people nowadays unfortunately prefer sin to obedience; they want to vent the anger that they feel in their hearts against their brothers, but they can't find any other way to do this except by gossiping. Shame on them for what they do!

# Types of Gheebah that are permitted

After discussing Gheebah in general, we will now explain the types of Gheebah that are permitted according to the Shari'ah.

BUT: beware that Shaytan may mislead a person to abuse these exceptions and take them as an excuse to do things that are forbidden, so that he may find himself gossiping constantly if he is not careful.

The types of Gheebah that are permitted are clearly defined and strictly limited, and such things may only be said when the intention is correct. There must be no motive to vent one's anger or to defame the person. Allaah (THE MOST HIGH) "knows (the tricks) that deceive with the eyes, and all that the hearts (of men) conceal."

The types of Gheebah that are permitted are as follows:

1 - Complaint - such as complaining to a ruler or judge.

The proof of this is the report of 'A'ishah (Allaah be pleased with her) in which she said: Hind, Abu Sufyan's wife, told the Prophet (peace and blessings of Allaah be upon him): "Abu Sufyan is a miserly man and does not provide enough for myself and my child, but I take from him without his knowing it." He said,

"Take what is sufficient for yourself and your child, and no more."

Further evidence can be found in the Hadeeth of Abu Hurayrah (Allaah be pleased with him), who said: A man said: "O Messenger of Allaah! I have a neighbor who harasses me." He said, "Go and put your belongings on the street." So the man went and laid his belongings out on the street. People gathered and asked, "What's wrong with you?" He said: "I have a neighbor who is harassing me; I told the Prophet (peace and blessings of Allaah be upon him) about it and he told me to go and put my belongings on the street." They began to say, "O Allaah, curse him! O Allaah, humiliate him!" (The neighbor) heard of this, so he came to the man and told him: "Go back to your house; by Allaah, I will not disturb you again.

2 - Seeking a Fatwa, such as telling the Mufti, "My brother - or so and so - has wronged me: how do I get out of this situation?"

This is what happened in the Hadeeth narrated above.

3 - Seeking help to change a wrong deed (Munkar) or to prevent a disaster that befalls a Muslim.

This can also be referred to the Hadeeth quoted above.

This includes the critical assessment of the reporters and witnesses in the transmission of Ahadeeth - this is to protect the authenticity of the Prophet's Hadeeth (peace and blessings of Allaah be upon him).

From Zayd ibn Arqam (Allaah be pleased with him), who said: We set out on a journey with the Messenger of Allaah (peace and blessings of Allaah be upon him), where we faced many hardships. 'Abdullah ibn Ubayy said to his friends: "Do not give what you have in your possession to those who are with the Messenger of Allaah (peace and blessings of Allaah be upon him) until they desert him. And in this case, when we return to Madinah, the honorable will drive out the meaner therefrom."

I came to the Messenger of Allaah (peace and blessings of Allaah be upon him) and told him about this.

He sent someone to 'Abdullah ibn Ubayy and he asked him whether he had said that or not. He swore an oath that he had not done so and said that it was Zayd who had lied to the Messenger of Allaah (peace and blessings of Allaah be upon him). Zayd said: I was very troubled because of this until this Ayah was revealed, confirming that I had spoken the truth: "When the hypocrites come to you..." [al-Munafiqun 63: 1]. The Messenger of Allaah (peace and blessings of Allaah be upon him) then called them to seek forgiveness for them, but they turned their heads away..."

Regarding this, Imam al -Shawkani (Allaah have mercy on him) said: The clear proof of that is the Hadeeth which was reported about al-Nasihah (sincerity) to Allaah, to His Book, to His Messenger, to the Muslims leaders, to their common people and their elites. Exposing lies and liars is one of the greatest forms of Nasihah, which is obligatory towards Allaah (THE MOST HIGH), His Messengers and all the Muslims.

He also said: Likewise, exposing a person who has given false witness regarding property, blood or honor is also a form of Nasihah which Allaah (THE MOST HIGH) has made obligatory on us.

From al -Sharid (Allaah be pleased with him), who said: The Messenger of Allaah (peace and blessings of Allaah be upon him) said: "If someone is able to pay his debt but does not, it is permissible to rebuke him severely and punish him."

Ibn Mubarak defined the punishment as imprisonment at the request of the one who is owed money.

Al -Munawi, in Qayd al-Qadir, also commented on this hadith and said that the harsh rebuke could take the form of the one who is owed money saying to his debtor: "You are an unjust (Zalim), you do not pay your debt on time," etc., but such reprimands should not include foul language or insults to his honor ('Ird). The punishment could be decreed by the Qadi to make him pay his debt, and could take the form of lashing or imprisonment.

5 - Consultation in matters of marriage, business partnerships or inquiries about a particular neighborhood (i.e., with a view to moving there) etc.

When both Mu'awiyah and Abu'l-Jaham asked for Fatimah bint Qay's hand in marriage, she consulted the Prophet (peace and blessings of Allaah be upon him) about them. He told her: "As for Abu'l-Jaham, he does not drop his staff from his shoulder, and as for Mu'awiyah, he is poor and has no money."

In another hadith, the Prophet (peace and blessings of Allaah be upon him) said: "Every Muslim has six rights over another:" It was asked: "What are they, O Messenger of Allaah?" He said: "When you meet him, greet him with salaam; when he invites you, accept; if he asks for your advice, then you should advise him..."

6 - Mentioning the sin of one who commits his sin openly, or the Bid'ah of the innovator.

No other faults of such persons should be mentioned unless there is good reason to do so, as outlined above.

From 'A'ishah (Allaah be pleased with him): A man asked permission to see the Prophet (peace and blessings of Allaah be upon him), who said: "Let him in! What a bad member of the tribe he is!"

Al-Bukhari concluded from this hadith that it is permissible to talk about sinners and those about whom one has misgivings in their absence.

From 'A'ishah who said: The Messenger of Allaah (peace and blessings of Allaah be upon him) said:

"I don't think so-and-so and so-and-so know anything about our religion."

AI- Layth said: They were two men from the Munafiqin (hypocrites).

7 - Description of a person known for a certain physical characteristic, such as al-A'raj (the one who walks with a limp), al -Asamm (deaf), al -A'ma (blind), etc.

It is not allowed to use these names with the purpose of insulting: if it is possible to identify a person by another name, then this is better.

From Usayyir ibn Jabir: The people of Kufah sent a delegation to Umar (Allaah be pleased with him), among whom was a man who made fun of Uways. Umar said, "Is there anyone from the Qaran tribe here?" The man (who had mocked Uways) came forward and Umar said:

"The Messenger of Allaah (peace and blessings of Allaah be upon him) said: A man will come to you from Yemen, and he will leave only his mother there. He will suffer from leprosy; he will pray to Allaah, and Allaah will cure him of it, except for a patch the size of a dinar or a dirham. Whoever among you meets him, let him ask for forgiveness for you."

Imam al -Shawkani (Allaah have mercy on him) said: If you ask me, "What if a person who had a nickname (Laqab) was not known by any other name?" I would say, "If that were the case, then that nickname would not be a nickname at all; it would be a proper name (Ism) by which the person is known, and he would not be known by any other name at all."

The specific Shar'ia cases outlined above have also been referred to in verse:

*"Criticism is not Gheebah in six cases:*

*Complaint, identification, warning,*

*Criticizing someone who is openly committing sin,*

*Seeking a Fatwa, and asking for help to correct wrongdoing."*

# Conditions that need to be taken care of in the case of the Gheebah which is permissible

You must have a pure sincere intention towards Allaah (THE MOST HIGH). Whoever mentions something true about a person, not to correct a fault but to discredit him, is a sinner. An example of such would be if a man asked another for advice regarding marriage, and the latter told him something true, not with the intention of revealing the facts, but because of some jealousy (*Hasad*) that he himself felt, so the person would not marry the girl in question.

This is *Haram* (forbidden); and there are many such cases.

2 - You should mention something that is true about your brother only if by doing so you will achieve one of the purposes outlined above and as long as you do not unnecessarily mention other of his faults.

3 - You must be sure that any evil that may result from this Gheebah will not outweigh its benefits and that it will not cause any Fitnah that may harm the Muslims.

# Repentance from Gheebah

It is necessary (*Wajib*) to repent after committing Gheebah, and you must hasten to turn to Allaah (THE MOST HIGH) and repent to Him, for none can forgive sins except Him.

There are four conditions that must be met when repenting from Gheebah:

1 - You must stop gossiping (or backbiting).

2 - You must regret what you have done.

3 - You must be determined never to do it again.

4 - You must ask your brother to forgive you for gossiping and pray to Allaah (THE MOST HIGH) to forgive you.

If you fear that some evil may result from your telling him, then it is not necessary to do so, and it will be sufficient for you to pray for him.

Ibn Katheer said in his Tafseer of Surah al-Hujurat, said: ... Others say that asking him for forgiveness is not a condition (of repentance for Gheebah), because if you told him about it, this may harm him more than if he didn't know about it."

Al-Nawawi (Allaah have mercy on him) said: "The Ulama said: If you have committed Gheebah , ask your brother for forgiveness." Commenting on this, our Shaykh al-Albani (may Allaah preserve him): "This is if you fear no worse evil in consequence of asking his forgiveness; otherwise it is enough to pray for him."

# Gheebah which is not recognized as such

1 - A man may mention something about his brother that he does not like, and when challenged, he says: "I am ready to say it to his face!"

This position can be rejected for the following reasons:

a. You mentioned something about him that he doesn't like behind his back - and this is Gheebah.

b. Being prepared to say it to his face is a completely separate matter. That doesn't justify you saying something behind his back about your brother that he doesn't like.

c. There was absolutely no need to say it behind his back if you were able to say it to his face.

d. You have no guarantee that he will forgive you for what you said behind his back.

e. It is clear from real life that being prepared to say something that a person does not like to his face is not a valid claim. This is Shaytan's way of deceiving you to commit Gheebah.

2 - In a gathering of people, when a person is mentioned, a man may say, "Alhamdulillah that we do not creep to the authorities!" or "I seek refuge with

Allaah from shamelessness!", or something like that. By saying this, he is both criticizing the other person and praising himself.

3 - A person may say: "Some people - or some of the Fuqaha, or some people we met - did such and such" - if the person he is talking to will understand exactly what he means by this.

4 - A person may be asked about his brother and may say: "May Allaah guide us, may Allaah forgive us, may Allaah guide him, we ask Allaah for forgiveness, we seek refuge in Allaah from evil," etc., so that it can be easily understood that he is criticizing him.

Likewise, a man might say, "So-and-so is only doing what any of us would do in the same situation."

5 - A person may sarcastically refer to another by using high-sounding titles, thus intending to insult him.

6 - A person might say, "He's young, we're allowed to talk about him."

That's a strange thing to say! There is no evidence that such a thing is allowed. There are no exceptions to the comprehensive prohibition of Gheebah; it is forbidden to gossip about anyone, old or young, male or female, rich or poor.

Why don't they say: "When the young gossips about the old, he does not sin?"

Why do they not remember the hadith: "The pens are lifted from three [i.e. their deeds are not recorded]: the sleeper until he wakes up, the one afflicted [by insanity) until he recovers, and the young boy until he grows up."

The Prophet (peace and blessings of Allaah be upon him) said: The pens have been lifted from three: the insane person who has no control over his mind until he recovers; from the sleeper until he wakes; and from the young boy until he reaches puberty.

7 - It may happen that Allaah (THE MOST HIGH) makes it easy for someone to enjoin what is right and forbid what is wrong in a difficult situation that no one else could handle, and the person addressed can respond by sincerely seeking to repent. But then Shaytan can mislead the one who gave the advice so that he starts telling the story to others: "So-and-so did such-and-such, but I advised him in that way ...".

What motive can there be for telling this to others, except one's own whims and love of gossip? Isn't the goal to "enjoin the right and forbid the evil" to spread the good among the people and stop the evil? So why talk about it when this goal is achieved? Or is it that whoever seeks to enjoin good is guided by Shaytan, and whoever seeks to stop evil falls into its trap?

8 - Being careless about gossip about a sinner.

This is not a clear case: It is not generally permissible. It is not permitted to gossip about anyone who falls into sin, otherwise it would be permissible to gossip about all the Muslims! Every believer commits sins - this is confirmed by the Hadeeth of the Prophet (peace and blessings of Allaah be upon him): "Every believing slave has a sin which he will commit time and time again or which he habitually commits and which he will not give up until he leaves this world. The believer was made to be tried, to repent and to forget, if he should be reminded and encouraged, he would repent and remember.

In another Hadeeth, he (peace and blessings of Allaah be upon him) said: "Every son of Adam errs constantly, and the best of those who err are those who repent."

How can they be so sure that it is permissible to gossip about the sinner? How do they explain the words "Your brother" in the Hadeeth: "Gheebah means that you say something about your brother that he does not like"? Does not this phrase cover both the righteous and the sinner?

How can it be different when the Messenger of Allaah (peace and blessings of Allaah be upon him) said: "The Muslim is the brother of the Muslim; he does not wrong him, he does not fail him, and he does not demean him. Taqwa is right here - and he pointed to his chest three times. It is evil enough if a man demeans his Muslim brother. Every Muslim is sacred to another Muslim: his blood, his wealth and his honor."

We ask those who take this matter lightly: is the blood of a Muslim sinner Halal? - Obviously not! So why is his honor not equally Haram when honor has been described, along with wealth and blood, as being sacred?

All this can be controlled by avoiding "mentioning anything about your brother that he does not like."

# Adverse results that may come from a careless attitude towards gossiping about the Sinner

1 - Rejection of guidance, refusal to accept good advice and hatred of those who call people to Allaah (THE MOST HIGH).

Unfortunately, this form of Gheebah is most often committed by those who frequent the mosques and seek to call others to Allaah (THE MOST HIGH). When they see a sinner, they start gossiping about him, whether he fails to pray or pay Zakat or to fast, etc. When these sinners hear about the gossip about them, they let it be known that they hate them, the ones who gossiped about them and that they cannot trust them.

Those who seek to call people to Allaah (THE MOST HIGH) and who frequent the mosques would do well to look upon these sinners with compassion and concern so that they may work harder to call them to Allaah, with gentle wisdom, so that they can be guided. How many Mushrikeen (polytheists), atheists and sinners used to spread corruption all over the world, but Allaah (THE MOST HIGH) guided them and they become the best of people with the highest morals... history amply testifies to this.

2 - Obstruction of reconciliation between conflicting parties.

It may be the case that a man gossiped about his brother, and when the latter heard it, he gossiped about him in revenge. When the first man heard about what the other had said about him, he took the matter further and spread gossip about everything the other man would hate to have said about him. The other man, in turn, would do the same. When people come forward to try to reconcile them, each of them will say, "But he said such and such about me, I can never look him in the eye"

All this backstabbing which contaminates the relationship between them is caused by ignorance and carelessness.

How often are these disasters and tragedies repeated in our communities! How many good relationships have been destroyed by that sort of thing! How many close friendships have been destroyed by this Gheebah!

Is it not time that these people fear Allaah (THE MOST HIGH), that their eyes weep, and that their Gheebah stop?

# Beware of gossiping about someone who is insufficient

Indeed, it is strange that we fail to help a person who is inadequate in some way, and even stranger that we harass him by gossiping about him.

On the authority of Abu Dharr (Allaah be pleased with him), who said: I said, "O Messenger of Allaah, which deeds are the best?" He said: "Belief in Allaah and Jihad (fighting) for His sake." I asked, "Which slaves are best (to free)?" He said: "Those who are most loved by their owners and who are the most valuable." I asked:

"What if I do not do that [i.e., release such a slave]?"

He said: "Help someone who is trying to do something or do something for someone who is unable to do it." I asked: "O Messenger of Allaah, what if I am unable to do anything?" He said: "Stop yourself from harming people, for this will be a *Sadaqah* (act of charity) from you for your own sake."

The Messenger of Allaah (peace and blessings of Allaah be upon him) explained to Abu Dharr who the best slaves were to free, and he explained how those who were unable to free slaves can also do good: that is, by helping one who is inadequate.

But unfortunately, the inadequate person is not safe from the evil of our tongue – we all criticize him, gossip about him and make fun of what he does.

# What is worse than Gheebah

One of the problems our society is currently facing is that we can see a man gossiping about his brother, not because of his sin or guilt but because of customs and traditions.

One of the unique attributes of Allaah (THE MOST HIGH) is that He alone is the Lawgiver who determines what is permissible and what is forbidden; this has nothing to do with traditions and customs.

An example of this is the case where a man may invite two or three people to a meal; one of his brothers (who wasn't invited on this occasion) might get upset so he starts gossiping about him just because he wasn't invited. All this is the result of ignorance and lack of religious knowledge. Where does it say that the man must invite you every time he thinks of inviting guests to a meal?!

If you want proof that such an attitude is indeed *Haram*, there is plenty of proof. But there is nothing but your own whims to support you.

Or a man may do something good which is encouraged by the Shari'ah, but due to ignorance of the rules of Islam, people will eat his flesh and his name will be constantly on the tongues of the ignorant and stupid.

For example, a man may be very modest in his dress, even if he could afford to dress well. Whenever the ignorant see him, they may say, "Look at this miser! Look at this man who has deprived himself of the enjoyment of this world! Look at this one who has made our religion dull and lifeless!"

Commenting on such people by saying things that are not true is very dangerous. People who say such things must be reminded the words of the Prophet (peace and blessings of Allaah be upon him): "... Whoever says something about a believer which is not true will be detained in Radghah al-Khabal (a kind of muddy swamp) until he can find a way to justify what he said."

Where are those whom the Prophet (peace and blessings of Allaah be upon him) described: "Whoever dresses modestly out of humility before Allaah, even if he could afford to dress well, Allaah will call him before all creation on the Day of Resurrection and let him choose which whatever garment of faith he wishes to wear."

It is our duty to love this person for the sake of Allaah (THE MOST HIGH) as long as he continues to be humble and have this good attitude and as long as we know that he is practicing Islam to the best of his ability.

First of all, we should find out why he does this, and we should think: is it Halal or Haram for us to speak ill of him, or to make an example of him and tell people: "He has made our religion dull and lifeless."

Allaah (THE MOST HIGH) will call him on the Day of Resurrection, before all of creation, and let him choose what garment of faith he wants to wear. But what will be your position on the day you who eat flesh and gossip about the believers? You will be in debt, full of regret and fear.

# Unspoken Gheebah

We are all too familiar with the Gheebah of the tongue, that is what is spoken, but Gheebah can take many forms.

Allaah (THE MOST HIGH) said:

"Woe to every (kind of) scandal-monger and backbiter."

[al-Humazah 104: 1]

From 'A'ishah (Allaah be pleased with her) who said: I said to the Prophet (peace and blessings of Allaah be upon him): "It is bad enough that Safiyyah is..." (Some of the narrators said: she meant that she was short). He said, "You have spoken a word which, if it could be mixed with the waters of the sea, it would have been." She said: "I imitated someone in front of him and he said: "I would not like to imitate anybody even if I were given such and such."

Al-Nawawi said: "... Likewise, any means that can be used to get the message across, such as imitating a person's walk, are Gheebah. In fact, they are worse than Gheebah, as al-Ghazali said: because they are more obviously understood and the meaning is much clearer."

Those people who mock others by imitating their walk, or way of eating or speaking, should fear Allaah (THE MOST HIGH).

The worst sinners today are the so-called "comedy films" where the actors put all their efforts into impersonating one person or another, in order to entertain people - no matter what fate these sins will lead them to. These sins include failing to raise children properly and raising generations whose careless and sarcastic attitude has no concern or interest in the affairs of society or the Ummah.

Unfortunately, these films are widespread, in cinemas and on TV and video.

May Allaah guide us to His path.

# Resisting Gheebah is the best of Jihad (fighting in the Way of Allaah)

Many people are surprised when they hear that opposing Gheebah is one of the best forms of Jihad, but their astonishment disappears when they hear the words of the Messenger of Allaah (peace and blessings of Allaah be upon him): "The Mujahid is the one who strives to control his ego (Nafs) in obedience to Allaah."

and: "The best thing about Jihad is that you strive to control your ego and your desires for the sake of Allaah (THE MOST HIGH)."

To keep oneself busy trying to prevent Gheebah is Jihad; it is actually one of the best forms of Jihad.

Jihad against the enemies of Allaah (THE MOST HIGH) can only occupy a limited period in a man's life, but the struggle to control the ego (Jihad al-Nafs) ends only when the man's life ends. And Jihad against the enemies can only be accepted from the Muslim as long as he also strives to free his ego from hypocrisy, tribalism and self-interest.

Every Muslim is obliged to strive to control his ego and prevent it from committing Gheebah; he must establish an Islamic state in his heart before it can be established on earth...

"On that Day the believers shall rejoice - with the help of Allaah. He helps whom He wills, and He is Exalted in Might, Most Merciful."

[al-Rum 30:4-5)

# Anecdotes of the Condemnation of al - Gheebah

1 - It is reported from al-Hasan al-Basri (Allaah have mercy on him) that a man said to him: "You have gossiped about me." He (al-Hasan) said: "You have not reached such a position that you can control my Hasanat (the reward from good deeds)!"

2 - Someone was told: "So-and-so has been gossiping about you" - so he sent him a dish of dates, with the message: "I heard that you had given me your Hasanat as a gift, and I will return the favor; excuse me for not being able to pay back the full amount..."

3 - It was reported from Ibn Mubarak (Allaah have mercy on him) that he said: "If I were to gossip about anyone, I would gossip about my parents, for they have more right to my Hasanat ."

4 - Gheebah is the hospitality of the wrongdoer.

5 - On the authority of 'Amr ibn al-'As (Allaah be pleased with him): he passed by a dead mule and said to some of his companions: "It would be better for a man to eat his fill of its flesh than of the flesh of his fellow Muslims."

6 - A man mentioned something bad about another to his friend. His friend said to him, "Are you going out and fighting the Romans?" He said, "No." His friend asked: "Are you going out and fighting the Turks?" He said, "No." The friend said, "The Romans are safe from you, and the Turks are safe from you, but your Muslim brothers are not safe from you!"

7 - If you are unable to do three things, then do three (other) things: if you cannot do good, then stop doing evil; if you cannot benefit people, then do them no harm; if you cannot fast, then do not eat the flesh of the people.

8 - The poet said:

"If a man is wise and fears Allaah,

This will keep him too busy to worry about other people's mistakes,

Just as the weak and sick are too preoccupied with their own pain, to think of the pain of others."

Reference:

Gossip and its adverse effects on the Muslim Community by Husayn al-Awayishah, translated by Huda Khattab